There's Hope in What We Do

THERE'S HOPE IN WHAT WE DO
Compiled and edited by Brenda M. Rider
Publisher, Philip D. Baden
Associate Editor, Vicki Matthews
Book Project Coordinators: Brenda M. Rider, Janeen A. Williams, Deborah M. Dashko, Karen S. Stilgenbauer
Cover artwork design: Janeen A. Williams

ISBN: 0-9765456-0-8

Second printing September, 2005.

A WAY WITH WORDS FOUNDATION
Board of Directors: Brenda M. Rider, Karen S. Stilgenbauer, Janeen A. Williams, Deborah M. Dashko R.N., William G. Reeves M.D., Thomas E. Himes

Special thanks to Dr. Reeves for keeping me (Brenda) around.

All rights reserved. All material copyrights are owned by the individual authors and used by permission solely for this book.

Printed in the U.S.A.

Forward

Thank you for reading this book. It's a collection of poems, stories, and heartfelt sentiment with regards to the big "C"... Cancer. Everyone who has submitted or donated to the book has been touched by cancer.

My name is Brenda M. Rider; I'm a cancer survivor and poet. With the help of a few friends we founded A Way With Words Foundation, Inc. It is a literary non-profit foundation. Through my cancer treatment and continued survival, I have used my ability to write to help myself and others cope.

The most common response after someone has read one of my poems is "you sure have a way with words". Because of this I knew what our Foundation would be called. Then we realized that there were many people in the area also touched by cancer that also had "a way with words". We decided to gather material getting the message out through word of mouth and flyers as well as mailings requesting submissions. We put together the project "Relay the Message". Paul Skowron, Janeen Williams and I collaborated on a song for the children of Tod's Children's Hospital to record. This group of children became the ROCcK (Raising Our Commitment for Cancer Kids) choir. The choir is comprised of patients, survivors, siblings and friends and together they became the ambassadors of the Relay The Message CD Project launched in May 2004.

This book contains all the material submitted to the CD project, and then some. Most of the material is poetry and other inspirations all with the thought "There's Hope In What We Do".

Brenda Rider

Some claim that "misery loves company". Others recognize the benefits of having an empathetic or sympathetic ear. Knowing that you are not alone in a tough situation can make a world of difference in your ability to persevere through the hard times. As social people we congregate into groups that love us, nurture us and support us. We turn to these groups in our times of need. We are also able to see how a positive attitude and the will to live, what we call the survivor's mentality can fend off even the toughest hardships.

If art imitates life, then this collection of poems, stories and thoughts in literary form is the purest essence of that survivor mentality. In its pages are found the bolstering words of inspiration, the soft touch of sympathy, and the silent embrace of understanding. Let the words soothe your soul and lift your spirit. Lose your self in its pages and come back to it periodically for an emotional booster shot. Above all, let the spirit of survivorship take root in your heart and flourish in all that you do. If this happens for you as a result of reading this book, then our collective hearts will smile as we welcome you to the fold.

Matthew Rider

Table of Contents

The Big "C"

Blessings 2
Remember October 3
Circle of Friends 4
Tears To Keep 5
One Day 6
Roses For Life 7
Relay For Life 8

Finding Your Way

Future 12
When Horses Run & Eagles Fly 13
Within You 14
Nature's Way 15
Birthday to Birthday 16
Life is Too Short to Wear Beige Pants 17

Tribute to Health Care

To a Yankee FAN-NY 20
Yankee Pride 20
Right Reasons 22
The Doctor's Wife 23
Angels Without Wings 24
Lighthouse of Hope 25
Best Nurse 26
Artist of the Spirit 27
Hope In What We Do 28

Dedicated to Heroes

Dandelions Roar 32
The Survivor's Life Saver 33
Light of a Child 34
Remarkable Child 35
Special Place 36
Christmas 2004 37

Family Circle

Grandma's House 40
The Rock 42
Brenda 43
What is a Sister? 44
My Country Girl 45
My Friend 46
Generation Bridge 47
Picked Up a Smile 48

Little Things

Classic Autumn Leaves 52
Art Show Colors Everywhere 53
Seeds For the Mountain 54
Holding Hands 55
Inspiration 56
The Tomato 57
For a Moment 58

Relay the Message CD

Body Mold 62
To My Father 63
Where's Maga 64
Walk Gently 65
Together 66
Sweetheart in Dreamland 67
One Step at a Time 68
The Token Song 70
Clear the Air 71
A Special Gift 72
Relay The Message 74
Dreams, Thoughts, Plans & Actions 75
Rainbow of Ribbons 76
Allie 77
Jessica 78
Someone's Watching 80
Eternity 81
Everlasting Faith 82
Faith 83

Many things inspire us.

Specific people or events inspired many of these words.

We wanted to share some of these inspirations with you.

Following many poems are notes of inspiration as shared by the author.

"The pen is mightier than the sword" is an expression we have all heard, at least once, in our lifetime. Word can be used to criticize, condemn, flatter, romance, outrage or inspire. Words can have a lasting impression on a person for life. A Way With Words Foundation, Inc. was created to leave a lasting impression of inspiration and hope.

Charlotte Labuda

The Big "C"

Blessings 2

Remember October 3

Circle of Friends 4

Tears to Keep 5

One Day 6

Roses for Life 7

Relay for Life 8

Blessings

I'm not the first or the last
To have my world move so fast.
Life changing decisions will be made
All seems lost, and I'm a little afraid.

It's difficult at times to look past today,
But the anger and tears are part of the way.
To ready ourselves for mountains to climb,
Knowing it's all just a matter of time.

There is always someone worse off then you.
They just keep smiling, knowing what to do.
Taking in stride the ups and downs,
Always looking forward not turning around.

For these people are the rocks where flowers grow,
A peaceful garden for they always know.
A faith as certain, as the day is long
Ready with a hand, steady and strong.

We may never realize the life we're liven
The blessings we have and gifts given.
How fortunate are we to have the flowers,
Maybe for the summer or a couple of hours.

There are survivors of cancer and life all around
Sharing their experience and strength they've found.
Life changing decisions have all been made,
With all the blessings I'm less afraid.

Brenda M. Rider
6-10-99

Remember October

In this world of pure creation
We're often left without explanation.

As to why we have a near life experience.
Though it's a battle with much interference.

October is the month for mammograms,
Doctor appointments and self-exams
.
A couple of hours set aside for her,
Everyone is racing towards a cure
.
Survival is measured from year to year.
Each one lessening a little of the fear.

With each journey we've had to face,
We proudly wear ribbons of satin and lace.

So this October take care of the livin,
And treasure the time and life we're givin.

Remember those who have reached higher ground,
For their spirit is felt all around.

Brenda M. Rider
10/24/00

Circle Of Friends

This circle of friends conquered their fears
Of what lies ahead beyond this year
Everyone there has something to contribute.

This circle of friends, that met every week
To draw on each others unknown strength
Gathered only to listen and try to cope
With their lives now touched with cancer & hope.

This circle of friends including the staff
Taught us to grow & cry even to laugh
They gave of themselves through experience music and art
But what they gave us most, came from the heart.

This circle of friends has helped us survive
And brought comfort to each of our lives.
The honesty & sharing that each person lends.
Allowed this group to be a circle of friends

Brenda M. Rider
3-5-94

After my Mom was diagnosed with lung cancer, my family and myself attended "I Can Cope" classes. This was my introduction to ACS and it's support system.

Tears to Keep

Things may happen without explanation
    A clear reason or causation.

A journey has started and problems are faced.
    Trotting along at a slow rapid pace.

I know you're worried when they enter the room,
    What could they tell us but impending doom.

We've done what they've said and said what they've done.
    Is it necessary to cry for more than one?

The anger you feel is long overdue,
    Though I wouldn't be better if it weren't for you.

The frustration that builds with each waiting game,
    Reminds us that life will not be the same.

As often are read prayers in a book
    I never understood the courage it took.

The thunderous sound of those deafening words,
    You need to cry and just be heard.

Symbolic of this time, a ribbon of pink,
    Circles around us a moment to think.

The tears that fall will warm your cheek,
    A cleansing of soul and spirit to keep.

Brenda M. Rider
1-17-00

One Day

In a short amount of time
Without reason or rhyme.
The road takes a drastic turn
Facing life's reality and patience learned.

It all happened within a couple of years.
When surviving is our greatest fear.
Every moment of every day,
Consumes our strength in a different way.

And the treatments continue,
To free what is in you.
Your spirit that never lacked.
Until one day.... You get your life back.

Relief is overwhelming as we smile once again.
Realizing our faith is from deep within.
The memories of these years will fade.
Then dreams and plans are finally made.

It all seems to happen one day
Somehow we always find a way.
To enjoy life with a brand new attitude,
And move forward again with such gratitude.

Brenda M. Rider
4-7-02

I wrote this for Rusty and Amy Boyles. Rusty had went through major surgery and treatment. He finally was given a clean bill of health, and they got their life back.

Roses for Life

A garden of flowers will often be
Beyond explanation to you and me.

In the garden of life a rose will stand
Soft to touch but not in your hand.

Flowers will bloom then slowly fade
Then bud again in brilliant shades.

With proper care and patience too
The rose you see is always true.

Enjoy the roses this early spring
A gentle reminder what nature brings.

Traditionally at special events
Their timeless beauty a moment spent.

Roses are fragile yet resilient each year
Much like the survivors gathered here.

Each one weathering the winter of their life
And celebrate now in the Relay For Life.

Brenda M. Rider
May 15, 2001

Relay for Life

Survivors have a common bond
A reality shared and courage found.

Symbolic first lap a circle with friends.
Giving us hope to begin again.

Survivors wish to participate,
Remembering those we dedicate.

Each single candle, a gentle flame.
Unite as one just the same.

Survivors prevail never alone,
But with another solid as stone.

Both will survive cancer and life,
A team event relay for life.

Brenda M. Rider
5-12-00

One of my Oncology nurses, Sandy B., described the Relay for Life to me. From this passionate detailed description I decided to participate in the inaugural Relay for Life in Austintown. I wrote the poem to be read at the Relay to commemorate this event. I was able to mark this event by reading it there on stage Bald and All.

"It's only cancer. There are worse things in this world"

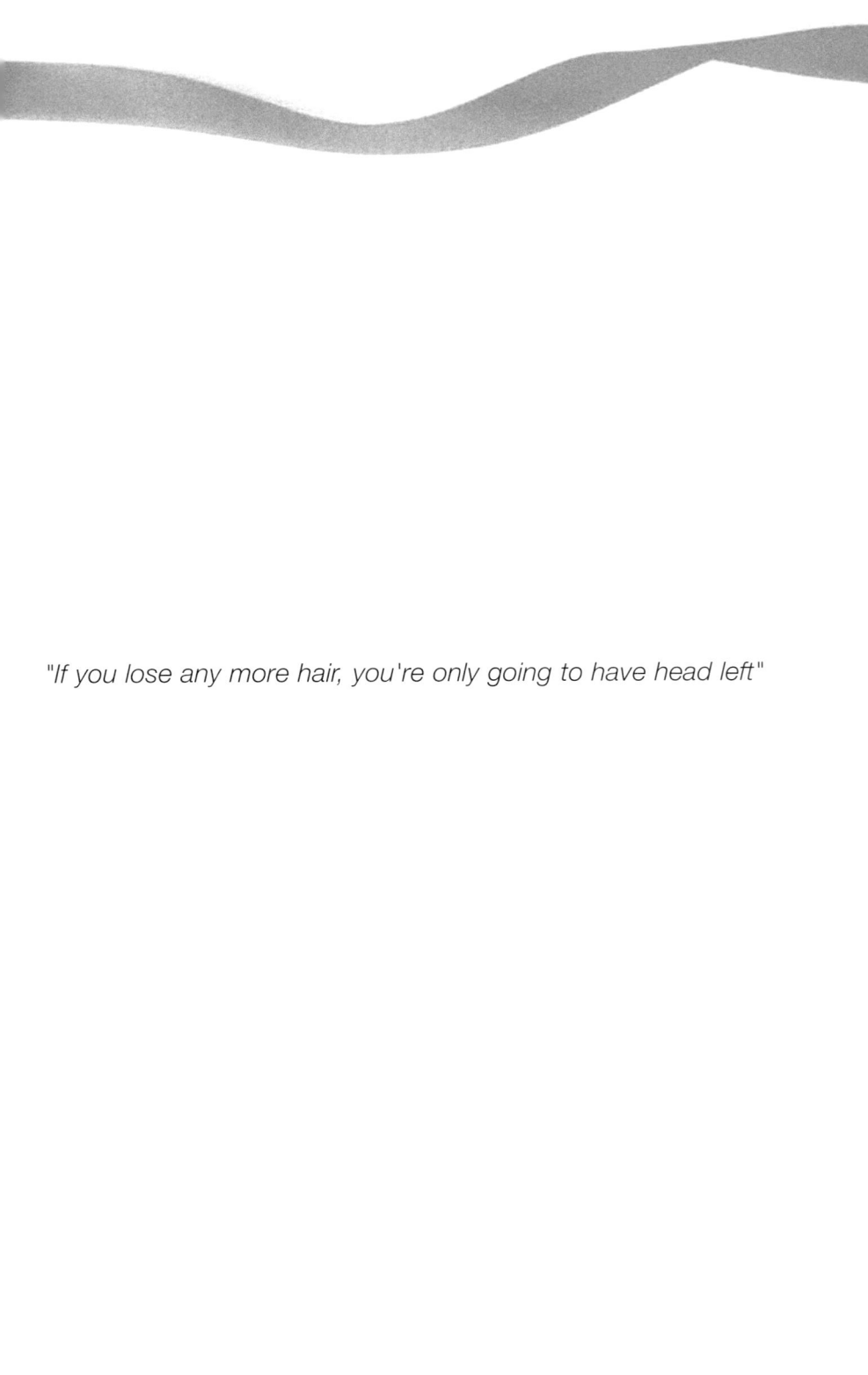

"*If you lose any more hair, you're only going to have head left*"

Finding Your Way

Future 12

When Horses Run and Eagles Fly 13

Within You 14

Nature's Way 15

Birthday to Birthday 16

Life is Too Short to Wear Beige Pants 17

Future

The fear of change is something you can overcome
I know it's easier said than done.
But learning to adjust to what comes your way
Makes living much simpler from day to day.

Not knowing what you'll do tomorrow
Maybe it's just a day you'll borrow.
Perhaps for a time to stand still
And let life go on, as it will.

The fear of change is not really the issue
It's the control you want, that might just miss you
The power to have your future in your hands
Frustrates you, as I know it can.

Not knowing what tomorrow brings
For you or anyone is the thing
Keeps us wondering in anticipation
Allows us to dream with expectation.

If you really think about what you cannot change
And accept that your life has re-arranged
Understand the importance of what is
And realize whose hands your future is in.

Brenda M. Rider
1-6-95

My Mom was feeling as if she had no control over anything. Not the cancer, not life, not anything. I wrote this to remind her, it never was in her hands, it's always been in God's hands.

When Horses Run and Eagles Fly

Many things in this world are unexplained
Why it happens isn't so plain.
Without knowing a reason why,
Horses run and eagles fly.

My circle of friends included me,
And grateful to them I'll always be.
One insisting every half year,
The other waiting, perhaps out of fear.

Whatever the reason we decided to wait,
The time came around and we made a date.
The three of us went, the morning was free.
To experience the world of mammography.

As fate would have it a lump was there.
Only for a short time I wasn't aware.
The results of the biopsy, its only cancer,
There's treatment available along with some answers.

The key to everything is how soon it's caught.
Doing what I'm suppose to, and not.
Whatever the reasons I don't know why,
Horses run and eagles fly.

Brenda M. Rider
5-27-99

Within You

Your spirit is a special force,
That you'll never understand
It lies deep within you soul,
I wonder if you'll let it run it's course

It will never settle down,
Just run free like a wild stallion
Looking for a prairie
And always flying high.

Let your spirit free
Let it find a simple me
Let it search for the reason
Of all the changing seasons
And the beauty I find within you...........
                within you.............

Maybe in the sunshine you'll find
All the happiness shining through
Or in the eyes of a child
All the wonder he sees in you.

Let you spirit free
Let it find a simple me
Let is search for the reason
Of all the changing seasons
And the beauty I find within you

Let your spirit free
Let it find a simple me
Let is search for the reason
Of all the changing seasons
And the beauty I find within you.....
              Within you.....   Within you......

Brenda M. Rider
1979

Nature's Way

Every garden needs the sun rays.
To warm the air on these cold days.
This brings the seed planted in just dirt
To blossoms then flowers, gifts from the earth

Along with the sun comes the violent storms
A clash of thunder & lightning cold & warm.
And just as quick the wind begins to rise.
Moving the storm on, clearing the skies.

Now the storm has past & the flower gets the rain
A much needed process in spite of the pain.
The flower is more colorful, & soft are its leaves.
As it grows further upward, swaying with the breeze

Every garden needs its storm to strengthen its roots
A time for growing the blossoms & fruit.
A way nature has of making things right.
Like the elegance of a butterfly prior to flight.

Brenda M. Rider

There are many things in life that are planted as seeds and we have to wait for them to grow. Sometimes time is all you need to see it through. This was written for encouragement for Karen.

Birthday to Birthday

Birthday to birthday another milestone.
Something achieved rarely on our own.

They have nothing to do with age.
A chapter ready to turn the page.

Birthdays are a state of mind.
Gentle memories of another time.

Birthdays are how one's life is measured.
With age comes wisdom and certain pleasures.

It's not the years one walks the earth.
It's the quality of soul, and what it's worth.

From our 1st. birthday we find our space,
To another birthday in a better place.

May each candle posses the warmth of the day.
And may you celebrate Birthday to Birthday.

Happy Birthday!
Brenda M. Rider
11-4-01

After battling cancer, every birthday is more important to you and everyone involved.

Life is Too Short to Wear Beige Pants

I once thought beige a safe sort of haven, something worn when nothing else would quite work. There is really safety in beige if you stop and think about it.

Beige doesn't scream, nor does it speak volumes about it's wearer. One blends in with the earth and can be ignored by the masses. No one will pester a soul in beige. They will most likely pass onto yellow, orange or pink.

Perhaps one wearing stripes or plaids have more to offer, more excitement or interest. Maybe a rebellious side, a burst of fun lurking from within, just longing for release.

As of today, I am disguarding all of my beige pants! Life is too precious to be that safe. Next week you will find me with purple and polka dots, and yes hortizontal stripes!

I surrender without reservation, wearing all things beige. I will save this earthy color for just that the earth! Yes that's it for the wheat field and the sand at the beach. For the sky just before a storm and for my cocker spaniel..Toby.

As for me the rules have changed-because "Life is too short to wear beige pants".

Sandy Bromley
11/2004

"Do what you can, and deal with the rest"

Tribute to Health Care

Yankee FAN-NY 20

Yankee Pride 20

Right Reasons 22

The Doctor's Wife 23

Angels Without Wings 24

Lighthouse of Hope 25

Best Nurse 26

Artist of the Spirit 27

Hope In What We Do 28

To a Yankee Fan-NY

Once upon a time in a land of Thrones
Was a potty called Little Grunt Groan.
Now Little Grunt wanted to be a champion commode.
Every season Little Grunt would flush and fill
Often under the same moon.
Every spring it was the same old crapper
They'd try for runs….Butt couldn't stop.
You see baseball is a strange past time
Each game different than the last time.
Every batter just wanting a little….hit that is a magical riddle.
Deep in the count at 3 & 2
The next batter up is overdue.
He takes a swing as if he meant it,
Hoping one day to bring home the pennant.
Then one day the "porcelain God" answered the phone.
And there was little grunt about to moan.
He'd been sitting there to push and push,
Soon he had a painful tush!
Then suddenly Little Grunt became a stinker,
And from there New York's greatest Thinker.
Steinbummer was his name
And the New York Tankees were in the game
Butt….the story doesn't end there.
They were champion commodes as seen here.
And New York went on to win
Every toilet bowl they got in.
The moral of the story behind every grand stand
Is a little stinker called a New York Tankees Fan.

Brenda M. Rider   8-20-01

Yankee Pride

I want to play ball like they did in those days,
Bat'er up, Bat'er up, pitch it to Mays.
Kofax was great as he whacked it outfield
Not the Sox nor the Braves, or even the Mets
Could hold back the Yanks or cause them to yield.

From The Babe to Jeter, fans will attest
No team shall be sweeter; the Yanks are the best!
Jolten Joe would be proud as he looks from above,
"My Yanks are so mighty, that team that I love"

Yes, I want to play ball like they did in those days.
But I like what I've seen from O'Neil and Tino
And Wow that El Duke` can never be beat.
Yes I like what I've seen and I don't like defeat.
So I'll wait and I'll pray and I'll ne'er take a bribe.
Just let me protest if I'm signed by the Tribe!

Yes I want to play ball like they did in those days
But I'll settle for now just to watch the Yanks sweep,
All those other clubs down, way down under their feet.
I will play ball with the big guys, not till year 10,
'Cause I know in my heart Yanks will "Sweep" even then.

Sandy Bromley a.k.a. Yankee Fan
10/1999

Oncology professionals are a unique group of people. The RN is responsible for administrating the chemo treatment necessary to kill off the cancer cells. They know how sick we're going to be, and the side effects we're likely to incur. Yet they keep us focus not on the miserable day to day but the big picture.

A large part of any healing process, is attitude and emotion. With me, I had plenty of both. Luckily, the oncology nurses who treated me had plenty of both also. Our friendly rival began between Sandy B. and myself. She had recently moved here from New York. I, of course, was a die hard Cleveland Indians fan. The friendly rivalry between the Yankees and the Indians was a way to communicate, laugh and tease. It definitely took my mind off the treatment.

The first poem Yankee Pride was written by Sandy B. to "rub in" the fact that the Yankees were in the playoffs and the Indians weren't. I wrote the second poem in the form of a children's story, Yankee Fan-NY.

Enjoy the poems and the deep sentiment attached.

Right Reasons

There are people in this world
Who ask nothing in return
For random acts of kindness
Sharing what they've learned.

We do it for a smile
It's own reward
Courage of a child
And all we're moving toward.

Will it ever get easier? Does it ever get tough?
To care for each other is more than enough.

Not expected or required
So inspired
Some always believe
Others struggle to achieve
To help a friend
Voices blend
The harmony was missing
Now we're listening.

Will it ever get easier? Does it ever get tough?
To care for each other is more than enough.

Everything we do. At every season,
Do it for all the right reasons….

Brenda M. Rider
1-4-03

Everyone knows that being a doctor can be rewarding financially. I have met a few who are doctors because they heal people, and help many others. These are the ones who do it for all the "Right Reasons."

The Doctor's Wife

A doctor is a tireless, noble man
Dedicated to saving of life;
But most have a silent partner
Known only as the "Doctor's wife."
She must always play second fiddle
To patients and a bottle of pills;
But always considering he took an oath
To fight all human ills.

A good doctor is always busy
With so little time of his own-
No set hours to end his day.
There is always the telephone
That calls him out at 2 A.M.
To treat Johnny or Mrs. Jones.
Does she envy the average housewife
Whose husband must be home?

Well, no way of life is free of care;
There is always turmoil and strife;
But your husband can't say, "Call back next week."
If it means a patient's life.
He would love to spend an evening at home,
Be a regular family man;
But a suffering world constantly cries
For his knowledge and capable hands.

So bless you lovely ladies
For having shared your men
With the hordes of sick and afflicted
To which there is no end.
May your patience be rewarded
In a new and better world;
But presently, may we just say,
"You're a special kind of girl.

Marvin C. Barrett (1976)

Angels Without Wings

God bless the caregivers, and the gift they give.
Helping the sick and those to live.
It may be as simple as holding a hand,
Till sleep arrives and we understand.

They are the ones who always smile,
Looking past appearances and all the while.
Ready with a kind word and a positive spin,
To pick you up when you need it again.

These angels without wings, soar beyond,
Till the gravity of uncertainty is gone.
Lifting the spirits to heights unknown,
Realizing that all of us may have grown.

The angels in my home all play a part,
Keeping me safe with joyous heart.
To face each day as a brand new thing,
God bless the angels without wings.

Brenda M. Rider
6-21-99

Lighthouse of Hope

With each passing day the body is healing
Clearing the mind, returning the feeling.
To absorb the experience of each new day.
Yes, I do feel better today.

Like the fog that lingers around daybreak
Shadowing the trees surrounding the lake.
Till the sun finally rises and the fog disappears,
The shoreline is there; it's all so clear.

During the darkness deep in the night,
On a distant shore burns a constant light.
A beacon of hope high off the ground,
Protecting the passing of those all around.

A lighthouse is built from brick and stone,
Situated there where wrecks are prone.
In sturdy form at the edge of a cliff,
Questioning the waves wondering why and if.

There's a light that's present in Oncology Care,
Visible to those who are willing to share.
Perhaps a dose of kind words or a smile,
That light can't be measured in nautical miles.

Brenda M. Rider
10-8-99

Best Nurse

A medical practice is a work in progress
A constant effort based on tests.

Not just one receives the recognition,
The unit shines with quiet dedication.

When you love what you do and do what you love
It's clear to all the guidance from above.

With Oncology nurses it's not about the accolades
But lives extended and friendships made.

A difference in one reward enough
In a work comprised of science and love.

With everyday things can get worse
It's only by chance you have the best nurse.

Among the chaos compassion and prayer
We're lucky to have the best nurses here.

Brenda M. Rider
2-6-04

This was in appreciation to the whole Oncology nursing staff at Dr. Reeves office. One of the nurses had won an award for going above and beyond and I thought they all, the entire unit, deserved an award for what they do everyday.

Artist of the Spirit

Artists of the spirit, nurture the soul
Replenish the well to reach another goal
Some artists paint with a brush, others with a pen
Some with words of wisdom rhyme with truth of friends.

Artists of the spirit play on a field of dreams
Realizing their heroes are closer than they seem.
They may appear, in a New York State of Mind
Or hiding in Cleveland for their turn to shine.

Whatever the situation the artists find the light
Perhaps wishful thinking felt with all your might
Encouragement with patience and a little jest
When to move & exercise and when to sit and rest

The artist of the spirit will always stand and lead
Sharing what is special to those who are in need.
They try to stay anonymous or just out of sight
But the spirit of the artist makes it all seem right.

Brenda M. Rider
1-3-00

Even though you may not have all you want right now, it will come. Always remember your time will come.

Hope In What We Do

In the spring of 2003
A Group of people gathered to be
Friends for life an event so unique.
The pictures say more than one can speak.

Compassion and pride to all who gathered
A celebration of life is all that matters.
Old friends and new share a title
"Survivor" of cancer has met it's rival.

The health care professionals present that day
Did more than healing in their own way.
A smile and laugh a warm embrace
Reached beyond a spirit on everyone's face.

Standing and watching as the camera took aim
Without the white coats we all looked the same.
With care close to home and friends so true
A journey of healing, there's hope in what we do!

Brenda M. Rider
4-8-03

Forum Health was shooting a commercial. It was a collaboration of survivors and cancer prfessionals. I was invited to take part. While I was there I was moved, because when you took the doctors and nurses out of their scrubs, we couldn't tell who was who – we were all the same.

"There is always someone that has it worse off than you do."

"Actions speak louder than words"

Dedicated to Heroes

Dandelions Roar *32*

The Survivor's Life Saver *33*

Light of a Child *34*

Remarkable Child *35*

Special Place *36*

Christmas 2004 .... *37*

Dandelions Roar

You've tried to defeat me
Tried to blow this flower down
But my roots are deeply seeded
Planted firmly in the ground

You wonder why I'm still standing
A sunny face among your yard
But you see I'm a survivor
Standing proud and standing guard.

Dandelions Roar!
When you think that you can beat us (Hey!)
Dandelions Roar!
When you try to tear us down (Ya!)
Dandelions Roar!
With our faces yellow shining
Yellow and shining toward the face
Of Our Lord
We've seen many dark hours
Our bodies fought far too many wars
But amidst the shots fired at us
These dandelions choose to roar

In a field of golden soldiers
Joined together hand in hand
Just try to blow us over
Because united we will stand.

Lori Neidlinger

A Cancer Survivor's Fight Song -
This poem was inspired by my Aunt Joann "Pink" Gainor who fought breast cancer for 9 years. She inspired so many people with her positive thinking and courage. I've always loved the sunny brightness of dandelions and couldn't understand why people didn't want them in their yards. They are also a symbol of strength to me. No matter what you do to get rid of them, they still pop up everywhere with their beautiful smiling faces. Through all the struggles my aunt went through with her cancer, I never saw her without her sunny face and her positive attitude. She was a true fighter.

The Survivor's Life Saver

When we learn to swim
We hang on to the side of the pool,
Or onto a life ring or another person.
Eventually we swim alone.

Living with someone who has cancer
Is like learning to swim
You hang onto each other
Until you can do it yourself.

I took care of my Aunt
Five years ago,
When she went through breast cancer.
Today we're swimming on our own.

Your Friend
Kaitlyn Dietz
Age 9

Light of a Child

A poem written by a wise young man
Tells about dreams, thoughts and plans.
"The look on a child's face,
Can take you to a happy place".

For Louis, life is about hope and dreams.
His and yours, and the time in between.
A brother, student, poet and son
To Chuck and Ann and Our Father above.

A true inspiration and Chicago fan
He touched so many without reaching a hand.
The beauty and sincerity in this child's soul
Can never be measured as hockey goals.

A candle will be lit to remember him
And just like a star the light never dims.
The higher the candle the greater the light
Louis is flying, no shadows of night.

Brenda M. Rider
4-7-04

This was written for Louis Hayes, who passed on at age 12. He was a charter member of the ROCcK choir, along with his brother Pete and sister Katie. Louis loved writing and was a poet who wrote well beyond his years.

Remarkable Child

On the wings of an angel, her spirit soars.
Reaching beyond to a peace ever more.

With God and family the courage she found
A remarkable child with love abound.

Just ask Jess she knows where it's at
From homework to sleds and all of that.

An organized person to every detail
Leaving instructions for all without fail.

She's a special gift to her Dad and Mother
But only one Ta-ta to her brothers.

The school she led in a cheer,
Knows she'll always be here.

A compassionate person everyone admires
Who taught you how to reach much higher.

With her wings this angel soars
At peace with friends forever more.

In memory of Jessica Moorhead

Brenda M. Rider

This was written for Jessica Moorehead, who passed on at age 16. She had an unshakeable faith, in God and others around her. This was true testament to her family and how she was raised.

Special Place

In my heart there is a special place
That only I can go
There's room enough for memories
And room enough for tears

I think of all those happy times
And your love I held so dear
Your smile, your hugs, your loving words
That warms away the tears.

In that special place of mine
I visit everyday
We can laugh and cry and talk
As the time passes away.

You are always there for me
In this special place of mine
To comfort, love, and protect
Until the very end of time.

Martha Zackeroff

*This poem is dedicated to my husband
who died of cancer three years ago.*

Christmas 2004

So often gifts aren't recognized
As presents in another ones eyes.
It sometimes takes a crisis or two
To appreciate what is in front of you.

This Christmas is special for many I know
A first for some, to find strength to grow.
An election year with Olympic gold
Mother Nature's wrath and stories untold

A series to break a baseball curse
Superman takes flight, and oil is worse.
Kids are moving, finding their own space
Others have moved to a better place.

Though Christmas brings all of us together
In person or spirit it always feels better
For distance can't measure the miles apart.
Yet Christmas lives all year in our hearts.

This year take time to discover your gift
And give it away without wondering if.
A difference made in the life of one
Is greater in the eyes of Our Father's Son.

Merry Christmas!

Brenda M. Rider

It's not a gift until you give it away.

"Live for today, you never know if there will be a tomorrow."

Family Circle

Grandma's House *40*

The Rock *42*

Brenda *43*

What is a Sister? *44*

My Country Girl *45*

My Friend *46*

Generation Bridge *47*

Picked Up a Smile *48*

Grandma's House

My childhood days hold memories
Of things both good and bad,
Like being poor and many things
That would make most people sad;
But I was blessed with riches
That some have never known-
Two kind and gentle Grandmas
That lived close to my home.

Grandma's house was a cozy place
With a fireplace warm and bright-
What a gratifying experience
To go there and spend the night.
Her beds seemed so much softer,
They smelled so fresh and clean.
Covered with beautiful hand-made quilts,
You could only have pleasant dreams.

Grandma's house was a happy place
Where people from far and wide
Stopped to rest and enjoy a meal
As they traveled the countryside
Bringing news from far away places
And interesting tales of old
Of ghosts with eerie faces
That could be guarding buried gold.

Grandma's house was a treasure chest
Of old and strange looking things
Like rocking chairs, a spinning wheel
And a porch with built-in swings,
A record player with a crank on the side
That played waltzes soft and sweet
And Grandpa's muzzle loader
Hanging over the mantle piece.

A pendulum clock chimed the hour of day
With a gentle rhythmic swing.
Grandpa's Bible with glossy prints
Of Jesus and sacred things,

Photo albums of long ago
When people dressed so strange,
And Grandma always had the time
To tell you all their names.

Grandma had many talents
Like growing beautiful flowers
Or a garden filled with produce
Where she toiled away for hours.
She could sew and mend your trousers,
Make little sister a dress:
But I think that Grandma's cooking
Was what we all loved best.

Anything she cooked was better
Whether boiled, baked or fried.
The more you ate; the more she glowed
With happiness and modest pride.
She seldom used a recipe or
Instant products of high esteem;
But when Grandma set her table,
It surpassed your wildest dreams.

There were biscuits like you never saw
And the most delicious pies.
Of all the cookies in this whole world
Hers would surely take the prize.
There were home-made jams and jellies,
Pickles, crisp and sweet,
Rare delicacies beyond compare-
Just all you could possibly eat.

Both my Grandmas have passed away
But in memory I still can see
Those pleasant smiling faces
That meant so much to me.
So, to you who have the privilege,
Don't wait until time has run out.
Treasured moments are awaiting you
Just over at Grandmas' house.

Marvin C. Barrett

The Rock

Momma had little education, a woman of modest means
But never went through life bitter, or gave up on her dreams

To me she was a rock, unaffected by mishaps in everyday life
She took the most pleasure in being a good mother and a loving wife.

She opened her heart and home to anyone who may be in need
It didn't matter a bit to her your race, your color or creed.

After daddy had passed on she didn't have the time to mourn
Standing strong and ever true weathering through each and every storm.

When her illness came upon her she didn't let it break her stride
Attacked it with true determination and her unbreakable pride.

Even while in the hospital she still took the time to care
For a new friend Hazel, that she met while she was there.

Momma took caring for Hazel like a proud mother hen
Yelling at the doctors and nurses, every now and then.

Hazel reminded me of a butterfly so tiny and yet so frail
She was full of vim and vigor although she was a little pale.

Meeting under the worst of circumstance they became instant friends
And remained true to their friendship until the very end.

My mother the rock began to crumble when Hazel passed away
The light that once filled her eyes faded a little more each day.

I will soon have to start facing all obstacles alone
That now will come my way
And remain unaffected by mishaps I may encounter each and every day.

As momma lost her exhausting battle that she had so valiantly fought
It occurred to me on that February morn…
Now it was my turn to be the rock.

Charlotte Louise Labuda June 27, 2002

> *My mother inspired this poem. Even at her lowest point, during her fight with cancer, she managed to worry and tend to others before considering her own well being. This has taught me a lot and I will strive to pass on all she taught me.*

Brenda

You came into my life
When there was such turmoil and strife
You gave to us then more than ever be said.
Even though you were in need, you helped us achieve.

Then as weeks turned to years, your presence ever near
We all learned a lot by watching you grow
With great determination and drive
You did anything you could which included, of course,
Things we didn't think you should
But most times we understood.

I found the man of my dreams and together we both know
Brenda's the one we should ask. She'll know.
How to make it or fix it or play it or get it.
Brenda believes we're all here for a purpose
Yours I believe is to make all of us grow.

You've always been Ant Ba, since I can remember
But NOW your Ant Ba to our littlest member
Elissa, like all the rest, loves and adores you,
She knows you're the one who's safest to turn to.

It's been 5 years for you since hearing those words
You've changed and you've grown throughout this whole fight
You've stopped, helped, and listened to the many or few
Who ever came calling or driving or knocking.

You've proven again that your strength is never-ending
You pick up and move on, but not over or down
Not Brenda, you climb, climbing ahead to things better
We don't know where we would be
Without you as part of our family

So here's to you, Ant Ba, The Brat, Brenda

You've given so much to each of us
We hope you know that we love you.
In ten years or twenty we can't wait to see
All the happiness you will be spreading each day

Vicki Matthews & Eric Matthews   May 7, 2004

What is a Sister?

What is a sister, but someone you can cry to?
Someone you can yell at, a friend you can run to
Someone who weathers the storms like a tall oak tree
The trunk standing tall while the branches move with the breeze.

A sister is someone who's been there all the while
Who's made you look, laugh and smile
A sister needs no invitation
Just to babble in idle conversation.

A sister is someone who always shows up
To encourage you to talk or just shut up
A sister is one who understands you best
Daring you to succeed test after test.

A sister at times is a mirrored reflection o
Of yourself, minus the imperfections.
A sister is a friend for life
So much like myself, I guess she's alright.

Brenda M. Rider
12/14/93

One year my dad wanted each of us to make for our sibling their gift for Christmas. This is what I did.

My Country Girl

My country girl, your beauty is perfection
A blooming rose a bright summer morn
Your sincere eyes show no sing of deception
My country girl your in a class all of your own
Your living arms hold me tight, when I need comfort
Assuring me no matter what that you'll be near
To strengthen me in success or any failure
My country girl these little things make you so dear
You've been content just to be a wife and mother
Stood at my side though all the hardships we have known
That is why for me there'll be no other
My country girl, I'm so glad you are my own

Marvin C. Barrett (1974)
Age 74

My Friend

I used to be all by myself
I was my own best friend
Never had anyone to love
Never had anyone to be my friend.

Then you came along
Like a rainbow after a storm
Chasing all my clouds away
Leaving behind only a love so warm.

Now every time I think of you
It makes me feel all good inside
And every time I look at you
I see all the love that you don't hide.

You shared with me a part of you
That doesn't often get shared
You are so warm and understanding
I find it easy to know you care.

Now I'm no longer all by myself
And you are my own best friend
I now have someone I love,
And someone who is my friend.

Brenda M. Rider
1981

Generation Bridge

There are pictures of your family tree
Relatively showing how the world should be.
Bearing a resemblance connected by genes,
Yes you're related even as a teen.

Each generation leaves a story behind
Of humble beginnings uncertain what you'll find.
The lessons learned of those before,
Leave open a window while closing a door.

Twice a child and once a man
Only words to understand.
For each generation a legacy grown
Reveals the hardship they have known.

Each in succession from one to another
Each believing the next will be better.
The Generation Bridge crosses many rough waters,
Grandparents to parents sons and daughters.

Brenda M. Rider
3/1/01

Each generation is different than the one before. Even though the times have changed, the struggles remain the same.

Picked Up a Smile

There are times when waiting is all one can do.
From one thing to another until it's through.
When the sun and moon share the same sky,
Reaching beyond without knowing why.

It's not often joy illuminates from a place.
Sacred and special shows on her face.
The patiently waiting for treatment to be done.
Now with plenty to do, oh what fun!

It seems as though the months lingered on,
She waited so patiently forever that long.
Then one day I was...Good As New,
Picked up the laughter and a smile too.

The excitement we shared in both of us
A leap of faith, quite a test.
A giggle and smile a gift to be,
Know the greatest things in life are free.

Brenda M. Rider
4/11/00

As I went through my breast cancer treatments, my 4-year-old niece, Kaitlyn, patiently waited for me to be able to play the way I used to with her. Once the treatment was done, and I felt better, more like myself, I walked in one day, scooped her up, and with that I picked up a smile.

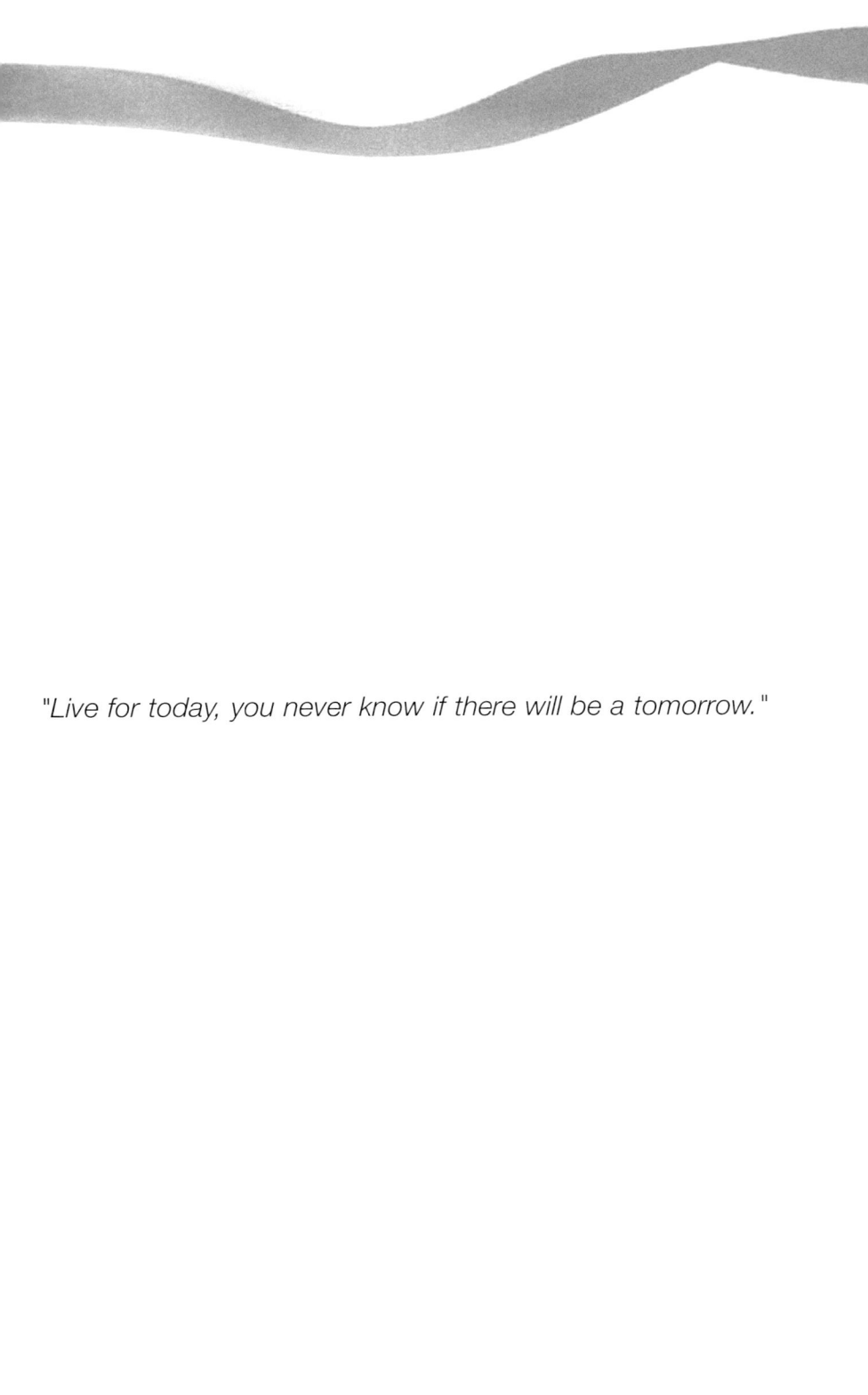
"*Live for today, you never know if there will be a tomorrow.*"

Little Things

Classic Autumn Leaves 52

Art Show Colors Everywhere 53

Seeds For the Mountain 54

Holding Hands 55

For a Moment 56

Inspiration 57

The Tomato 58

Classic Autumn Leaves

Around the tenth month of every year.
The winds of change arrive here.
Bringing forth, a cool breeze.
Catching the leaves from tree to tree.

The colors explode into the sky,
Against the clouds not knowing why.
Gently fall like mornin rain.
All of this can be explained.

Each year is better than the one before.
Leaving you dreaming on a distant shore.
The mountains have met the oceans of blue,
And the change that occurs will comfort you.

The shorter days and evening frost,
Remind us of the last pitch tossed.
For each fall is a classic one,
The autumn leaves are never done.

Brenda M. Rider
10/17/00

One Fall as I was driving my Dad to treatment for his prostate cancer, we both noticed how spectacular the changing leaves looked.

Art Show Colors Everywhere

Fall's in the fresh air
The harvest now here.
Color is everywhere,
Green peppers, red tomatoes, yellow squash.

That's not all,
God's Art Department
Working overtime.
Look! Color's everywhere.

Every color under the sun and shade.
Leaves bright yellow, cherry red,
Pink and golden amber.
Colors everywhere!

You are invited to the
Greatest art show on earth.
No ticket required,
Any old park bench will do.

Thomas P. Gilmartin
From *Back to Basics II*

Having cancer is not a pleasant thought. Think before you act. The human body can get very sick and make a recovery. The message here is "Don't Give Up." Not always, but sometimes it's up to you.

Seeds for the Mountain

Natures elegance there in a sun rise
Peaking over the horizon piercing your eyes.

Picture a land where the sun never sets.
The moon and mystery often forget.

If the moon never rose and the sun never set.
How dormant our lives would get.

Off in the distance a mountain range,
Each season's reward is often change.

The enormous presence of heavens perch.
Allows you to blossom and continue the search.

Once you've reach the mountains peak
A climb for strength not for the weak.

Each day is filled with highs and lows
Revere the challenge.... lookout below!

Much like our lives in recent years
It's difficult not to hide in fear.

To boldly walk down the other side
And keep the faith deep inside.

Once on top you stand to lose
The mountain and splendor left only to view.

The valleys between, not rejected you know
Just a better place for seeds to grow.

For Karen   10-31-01
Brenda M. Rider

There are many things in life that plant as seeds, and we wait for them to grow. Sometimes time is all you need to see it through.

Holding Hands

Whatever happened to
The practice of holding hands?
Is it right or even polite?
Have you ever watched a movie
Or a play holding hands?

When taking a walk or
A stroll, isn't it better
To be holding hands?
We still shake hands, hug
And even kiss, but
Whatever happened to holding hands?

Holding hands is a lost art
That should be revised and
Encouraged by young and old.
Try it, you will find it
To be a tantalizing experience.
May I hold your hand?

Thomas P Gilmartin Sr.
From *Back to Basics II*

Having cancer is not a pleasant thought. Think before you act. The human body can get very sick and make a recovery. The message here is "Don't Give Up." Not always, but sometimes it's up to you.

For a Moment

The other day I noticed something in the grass
An orange & black butterfly & I had to ask.
How is it I happened to notice this beautiful little creature
It's brilliant colors & delicate little features?

I stood there for a moment as if time stood still
Waiting for it to move, as I knew it will
For it only stopped a moment to heal a broken wing.
It's freedom somehow threatened among other things.

So many things in life can bring about tears.
From simple joy, to hiding one's fears.
For this butterfly it's routine has changed
Like much of your life is not the same.

Just like the butterfly I saw in the grass
Vulnerable to the world, when someone walked past.
It's only natural to be angry and scared.
But realize you're not alone, and of those who care.

I stood there for a moment as if time stood still
Waiting for it to move, as I knew it will
Just like this beautiful butterfly with it's broken wing.
I know too one day you'll fly, among other things.

Brenda M. Rider
10/10/97

A friend Louise Stovall, was going through breast cancer treatment. She was dealing with all the changes without hesitation. This poem was a little encouragement. Eventually, after all the changes you will emerge like a butterfly out of it's cocoon.

Inspiration

On days when fatigue, depression self pity have consumed our lives
Like the black ominous clouds of a thunderstorm
You've taught us to see the sun and rainbows
Hidden just beneath the surface

On days when it takes every ounce of energy we have
Just to get out of bed
You've proven your strength is greater by simply putting on a smile
And facing the world head on.

On days when we complain about how the wind
Has been blowing our hair around
Or that we have forgot our sunglasses
You've taught us to appreciate the little things, like eyelashes and hair
Aren't for just holding mascara and hair spray.

On days when our biggest fear is breaking a nail or
Fitting in our favorite jeans
You've taught us that fear can be overcome by having patience,
Showing others compassion and understanding,
And believing in the power of prayer.

On days that we waste precious moments
Complaining about how time seems to be standing still
Only to complain about how fast it seems to fly by
You've taught us that fear to appreciate not the quantity of time
But the quality of life.

Your strength and determination through the years
Have been a true inspiration to all those who know you
You've taught us to appreciate life as a whole a little more each day.

You've taught us so much, what could we do, as mere peons,
To possibly help you when you've had one of those days?

Charlotte Louise Labuda Age 40
March 3, 2000

This was written for a friend of mine who is a breast cancer survivor. Her strength and determination is never-ending. She is truly a great inspiration not only to me but also to everyone she meets. She is a great advocate in educating the community about cancer and the research that is available.

The Tomato / Life Relationship
"Comparisons"

When I was born the seed had already been planted. Kind of like a tomato as its tender green leaves gently push thru warm soil in the spring. As a baby I am tender and green as well, unaware what direction life has in store.

Shall I thrive or shall I be weak and willowy, even allowed to exist. Shall someone devour me with love and nurture me, provide just the right enviroment? Fertilize me and watch me grow. Yes I think I'm like a tomato, always have.

Now a toddler, my stems are getting stronger. I stretch and explore always try to bounce toward the light. My nourishment continues as I grow reaching always searching. My roots are fixed. Will they support me through the dry spells, the rains or will they shrivel and collapse?

For my pre-pubescence I sense awkward twists and turns. The fruit is stirring, waiting to burst forth. Seeds are there growing but not quite ready. There is doubt and concern but I do not know what to do with it just yet. As the vine grows and strengthens, so does my soul. The sun continues to drench over me, warms me, makes me feel safe.

My womanhood is upon me again there is stirring within me, but this time I know why. The seeds have matured and the fruit is about to show it's youthful face. I am happy to know these seeds can multiply and carry on as nature always has. God willing will continue to do so.

As a mother I watch my offspring from the branch that once was my own. Now it's their turn to reach for the sun and enjoy it's warmth. Now they grow, the process, the natural progression, the order. It is the plan.

My fruit is beginning to wither, the ripening completed, all picked, all spent. The seeds are gone as the vine shrinks. I ponder my past, what have I done in the life that started from a seed planted so long ago.

Now well past my prime my aged and shriveling shine once youthful, supple, shows itself. The warmth of the sun still shines upon me but does no good, serves no purpose. My time is done here on God's good earth. Not much left to offer now except for my roots. They stay strong and unshaken. The seeds are forever gone except for valuable few that now flourish before me. Their time is now, their vines are growing, thriving and reaching for the sun. With proper love and nourishment, the right balance of fertilizer they too will grow and cast the seeds received from me.

So you see, life is a lot like a tomato.
I have always thought that.

Sandy Bromley
11/2004

Relay the Message
CD Material

Body Mold *62*

To My Father *63*

Where's Maga *64*

Walk Gently *65*

Together *66*

Sweetheart in Dreamland *67*

One Step at a Time *68*

Token Song *70*

Clear the Air *71*

A Special Gift *72*

Relay the Message *74*

Dreams, Thoughts, Plans & Actions *75*

Rainbow of Ribbons *76*

Allie *77*

Jessica *78*

Someone's Watching *80*

Eternity *81*

Everlasting Faith *82*

Faith *83*

Body Mold

Our bodies are formed by genes and cells
But our minds are formed by something higher than our selves
We grow and we learn by each passing day
And we learn acceptance by the life God gives us, I pray

One morning I woke without a single step
My legs would not move and I had breakfast for my son to prep
I couldn't walk… I couldn't even get out of bed
What is happening? My mind began filling with dread

My partner came home for lunch that day
I told her about my legs so she decided to stay
She took me to the hospital and they ran all tests
They weren't able to find why my legs took a rest

I was sent home in a wheelchair to tow
I still wasn't walking and no one had a reason to show
When I was lifted into our one story home
My right leg slipped off the rest and broke at the hip bone

They rushed back to the hospital to find
That my breast cancer had struck my bones this time
Acceptance is hard to do when you're scared
Of losing your life without another day for, my son, to care

As a child mom said that they broke the mold
And I learned that everyone came from their own body mold
And that each one is different in shape and size…
That God made us all for a special purpose in life, I surmised

Life is a gift to cherish each day
And to remember the simple things that come our way
I have to fight this disease that has entered my body
But I can do this with God almighty!

Judith Campbell

To My Father

Written in memory of my father, Paul Repko,
who died March 15, 1993.

A kinder, gentler man you could never find.
He lived his life through his deeds -
Helping family and theirs - always.
There will be an eternal void in
Everyone's life who knew him.

He never bragged - he moved the train by
The engine - not by the whistle.
God has a special place for him in heaven
And he is looking down on us with love.

We never needed outward gestures of
Our love for each other – it went
Deeper than that – But I always knew
I was "Daddy's Girl."
Someday the pain will ease, but you
Will live forever in my heart Dad.

Karen L. Schaffert

Where's Maga

Where did my Maga go, I need to know where she went
She has left with the angels that the good Lord had sent

Why did she leave so quickly, I still need her here
I try to be comforting and ease all of their fear

She's not really gone I say to them, just simply look around
She's the butterfly on the wind; she's the penny on the ground

She's the unexpected gentle breeze you feel on the hot summer day
She's the rainbow that appears after the storms have all gone away

We can pass on her legacy remembering all that she had taught
Remembering all the sacrifices she had made for us all the battles she fought

Try to be loving and kind and in God you should place your trust
Give others the benefit of the doubt of this you know is a must

To truly give of ourselves when we have nothing left to give
Always be caring and gentle and show others what it really means to live

Give your love unconditionally to every girl and boy
The simple things are always best and will bring you the most joy

Open up your heart and home to anyone who may be in need
Treat everyone with the greatest respect no matter the race, color or creed

Learn to roll with the punches and take everything in stride
Live your life to the fullest and treat it with the greatest pride

"Maga" is always close by, she's never too far away
She's watching over all of us every night and every day

Charlotte Louise Labuda
June 14, 2002
Age 40

The unfortunate passing of my mother from her bout with Cancer inspired this poem. This is how I helped explain the loss to my son and taught him some lessons I learned from her along the way.

Walk Gently

When I close my eyes
I go to my secret place
The door opens
I see sunshine and bright colors
I smell flowers and touch birds
I run to catch sunbeams of
Flitting butterflies
I feel peace and the soft caress
Of my surroundings
I feel a gentle hand of assurance
For someday my eyes will be opened.

Martha Zackeroff

I was inspired to write because of the article about Jessica Moorhead. I sat down and started to write and within minutes I was finished. The words were given to me. She was an inspiration to many people, I found it difficult to talk about cancer and writing this poem has helped me come to terms with my own battle with breast cancer. I am a four-year survivor.

Together

Together, my friends, united we stand
We'll fight a good fight and stand hand in hand.
Together my friends we'll find the way
With love and support, a victory each day.

The strength that we show or the knowledge we share
Can make a person grow and gives us the passion to care.
The path we choose includes family and friends
Keeping faithful watch, we can always depend
On those who surround us and love us for us.
They give us support without judgment or fuss.

The course we choose to take through life
Is often filled with triumph and strife.
Can the path we choose to lead each day
Change the lives of others?   It may.
Did you know you can change the world?
Of course you did, or so we were told.

And in the end, you know how we'll be known,
The family we choose, and the courage we've shown.
Did I change the world? You bet I did.
I changed it each day I opened my lids.
Can you imagine anything more profound in the end?
To change the world by being a great friend.

Together my friends we'll find the way,
With love and support a victory each day.
We'll fight a good fight and stand hand in hand.
Together, my friends, united we stand.

Vicki Matthews
4/15/03

Sweetheart In Dreamland

I stayed home last night as I often do
To keep a date in dreamland with you.
It's a make believe world where I lose track of time
Enjoying each moment that you're only mine.

Real love is disappointments, heartaches and despair!
My world is happiness tender love and care.
Though I may never kiss you or even hold your hand
You're my perfect sweetheart when we meet in dreamland.

Marvin C. Barrett (1970)
Age 74.

One Step at a Time

Don't close your eyes, there's so much to see
I've waited so long
You're finally standing here with me

Take it all in
Don't miss a thing
Keep up the pace with me
We'll make it to the end

We are free to fly away from here
Sail above the world
And change all fear into love
For everyone to see
You and me, taking it one step at a time

All the faces next to me
Frees my mind from doubt
The stars above and the candles below
Remind me what life is all about

We've got the stars on our side
Through our walk in the night
I can see hope on each face
I see love in this place.

We are free to fly away from here
Sail above the world
And change all fear into love
For everyone to see
You and me, taking it one step at a time

Don't close your eyes, there's so much to see
I've waited so long
You're finally standing here with me
For everyone to see
You and me, taking it one step at a time

Tristan Ula

This song was written after experiencing the Relay For Life as a committee member for my high school. When I saw the candles around the track and the candles in the stands, it gave me so much strength to keep walking. I watched the survivor's walk and the closing ceremonies that year and they were incredibly moving. I imagined someone saying " C'mon, you can do it, keep the pace with me, take it one step at a time."

*Accompaniment
Bryan Stefek*

Tristan came to me with the lyrics to a song and wanted to finish it for the Relay For Life. I quickly helped her. Then a year later, when we were recording the song for the Relay The Message CD Project, I was amazed to find so many different artists from different genres writing songs and poems for the same cause. The song that I helped to write wasn't my song anymore, it never was, it belongs to these people. All of those who have made it through cancer, died trying, have it and will have it are now and will always be an inspiration to me. I feel honored every time I play "One Step At A Time," because I know that my fingers are playing for all of these people.

The Token Song

The parking lot-hospital parking lot
Don't forget your token for the parking lot
It'll make you scream and holler
'Cause you'll have to pay a dollar
If you forget that little token for the parking lot.

One day when I was leaving after a treatment was done
I need not tell you treatments aren't much fun
When I finally got to my truck
I realized I was out of luck
I forget my token for the parking lot.

The parking lot-hospital parking lot
Don't forget your token for the parking lot
It'll make you scream and holler
'Cause you'll have to pay a dollar
If you forget that little token for the parking lot.

And then there was the day
An embarrassing one I'll say
I tried to put the token in to the slot
But it fell to the ground
And was no where to be found
I couldn't get out of the parking lot

The parking lot-hospital parking lot
Don't forget your token for the parking lot
It'll make you scream and holler
'Cause you'll have to pay a dollar
If you forget that little token for the parking lot.

Debbie Woodford

Throughout my treatment for breast cancer I "battled" the parking lots of Trumbull Memorial and Northside Hospitals.

Clear the Air

And when you're challenged, stand up strong
You're blessed with strength to carry on
You were forced to fight you will…with will to survive
You are heroes of the land, spangled cross the skies
Shallows ignored you, Science explored you, I implore you!!
Don't let the nightfall frighten you.
Warm rays of sunlight will shine through
The imperfections we all share, we'll wear with pride
Show one another we all care, then
Let's go outside and clear the air.
Become aware……show that you care….

Yes I can continue all my plans
I pledge to make all of my dreams come true.
Hand in hand and gentle as a lamb
We will triumph one and all and march through what we have to do
Yes I can continue all my plans
I pledge to make all of my dreams come true.
Hand in hand and gentle as a lamb
We will triumph one and all and do what we have to do

Yes I can continue all my plans
I pledge to make all of my dreams come true.
Hand in hand and gentle as a lamb
We will triumph one and all and march through what we have to do
Yes I can continue all my plans
I pledge to make all of my dreams come true.
Hand in hand and gentle as a lamb
We will triumph one and all and do what we have to do

Ron Gianoglio
Aug 2002

I was inspired through many stories and tales of both sorrow and joy.

A Special Gift

Children with cancer
Are a special gift,
Filled with love and joy
And the hope to live.
They cherish each day
And pray ev'ry night
That everythin's
Gonna be all right.

They tell their stories
To people all around,
Of the love and care
That they have found.
And whether these stories
End in happiness or despair,
They're heartfelt teachings
Move people everywhere.

Children with cancer
Are a special gift,
Filled with love and joy
And the hope to live.
They cherish each day
And pray ev'ry night
That everythin's
Gonna be all right.

They always support others
And lend a helping hand.
If you have a problem,
They'll try to understand.
They've walked a weary road
And fought wars along the way.
They've earned their battle scars,
But they're standing here today.

Children with cancer
Are a special gift,
Filled with love and joy
And the hope to live.
They cherish each day
And pray ev'ry night
That everythin's
Gonna be all right.

Children with cancer
Are a special gift,
Filled with love and joy
And the hope to live.

Hilliary Hill
Age 13

My family and my own experiences have inspired me to write these lyrics. I would like to share my experiences with people around the area. I hope to inspire those who hear my lyrics.

Relay The Message

Within the walls of a healing place, Life so precious grows
Innocence there on every face, So much more they know.
Just a dream a survivor holds....sprinkled with faith...

Never giving up, on ourselves or you. Trust without a doubt.
Remember what it's all about, There's Hope in what we do.

We all dream of another day, when the sun will rise…if only to play
Look to the children, a gift from above, they teach us the way with love.
Just a dream a survivor holds…..Sprinkled with faith……

Never giving up, on ourselves or you. Trust without a doubt.
Remember what it's all about, There's Hope in what we do.
Relay the message, Relay the message, Relay the message

Understand what you did for me, gave me strength to carry on….
Never giving up, on ourselves and you. Trust without a doubt
Remember what it's all about. There's Hope in what we do.
Relay the message, Relay the message, Relay the message

There's Hope in what we do.

Brenda M. Rider

This poem, now a song, has become the ROCcK choir's anthem. They have taken this song and made it their own.

Dreams, Thoughts, Plans and Actions

As life grows longer
The days creep by
And all of life
Begins to die
But what one sees
In a child's face
Can change one's life
To a happy place.
For vision and dreams
A regret to have
As you live your life
On your own set path.
A child's soul can make ones day
A time of life
And a time to play.
The child grows older
The dreams grow large
And life becomes
An endless barge
Of plans and wonders
That must be tried
And plays and wonders
To be applied

Louis Hayes
12-23-02
1:00 A.M

Rainbow of Ribbons

A rainbow is a promise, for all the world to see.
Faith as a picture, of God's true beauty.
A rainbow of ribbons, we choose to wear.
Unifies a people, showing that we care.

Those who are survivors, and those the reasons why.
Carry a promise with them, everyday that passes by.

Ribbons displayed for county or cure.
Color the intentions, both honest and pure.
It may be a disaster, or a battle hard fought.
A victory perhaps, a lesson taught.

Those who are survivors, and those the reasons why.
Carry a promise with them everyday that passes by.

Each candle that's lit around the track.
Brightens a soul wherever it's at.
A community that rallies, for so many hours.
Oh the dedication, feeling his power.

And those who are survivors, and those the reasons why.
Go hand and hand with us, long into the night.
A rainbow of ribbons, a rainbow of ribbons,
A rainbow of ribbons.....Relayed for Life.

Brenda M. Rider
11-19-01

After 9/11, I noticed everyone wearing different color ribbons for various reasons. The patriotic colors, yellow for troops, pink for breast cancer, and many others. The people were survivors of life, cancer, and various causes.

Therefore, a "Rainbow of Ribbons" (The Survivors Song).

Allie

I see her siting by the window in the bedroom
I break down because I know she isn't there
My father tries to be strong I hear him crying in his room
That's OK I know how hard it is to bear

I know it can't be true, but what do I do
Allie
I hold her so near, butt she's oh so far away
Allie
I see her. I feel her. I love her and I miss her
Allie
If I could hear her, She'd say I'll hold you close again someday
Allie

I smell the ginger wafting from the stove
She loved to bake for me. I can almost taste it now.
I lay awake and I feel cold air coming in
I feel her tuck me in but I don't know how

I know it can't be true, but what do I do
Allie
I hold her so near, butt she's oh so far away
Allie
I see her. I feel her. I love her and I miss her
Allie
If I could hear her, She'd say I'll hold you close again someday
Allie
I miss you I can't bear to live without you.
Allie
I see you. I feel you. I love you and I miss you
MOM
If I could hear you, You'd say I'll hold you close again someday
I see you. I feel you. I love you and I miss you
MOM

Will Fithian and Theo Kennisten

Jessica

Do you know just how long the river of love is?
Can you see what it means to be amazing?
Would it help you to see the awe that I'm feeling?
If I summed it up in just a name
I don't know how one can stand beside you
And not feel loved and warm and real.

Jessica
Can you hear me?
You're always near me
There's a power to your love.

A little girl some may say till they're near you
Will they hear you? The words are years away.
I'm so glad I know you.
You've opened eyes and opened doors without even trying
Through it all you've only just been you

And that smile, if I could put it in a bottle
I could buy and sell this great big world a million times or two.
Children adore you. They sense a calm within you
And as for me, I chose to watch and learn.
Jessica
Can you hear me?
You're always near me.
There's a power to your love

A little girl some may say, You're a giant
And everything you do it comes from love they say
I'm so glad I know you
Jessica

I look up to my sister
What I see is good
I love you
And I wish I could have the power to heal you
Today, Yes I would
You are the love
You are the good
You've taught me so much
You mean the world to all of us
Jessica

Do you know how long the river of love is?
I think I do because I see it in you

Jessica
Can you hear me?
You're always near me
There's a power to your love

A little girl some may say, You're a giant
And everything you do it comes from love they say
I'm so glad I know you
Jessica

Paul Skowron

Someone's Watching

When a lonely voice calls
When a single tear falls
There is someone watching over you.

When you're tired body's aching
So bad your heart is breaking.
There is someone watching over you.

When your strength is disappearing
And it seems nobody's hearing
There is someone watching over you.

To help make your burden lighter
And your outlook so much brighter
There is someone watching over you.

Sometimes we have to fight the battle
When fighting seems impossible to do
It's good to know that there's an angel by your side
And as sure as heaven you will get through
You'll get through

You could say with pride you beat it
Went the distance to defeat it
There is someone watching over you.

Now the world is at your feet
And life has never been so sweet
There is someone watching over you.

Eric McClellan

Eternity

My life began like any other
In the heart of my dad and the arms of my mother
They taught me prayers and read stories of a child much like me
And our father in heaven that I cannot see

I learned as I grew about faith, hope and love
And that God gave these gifts to each and every one of us
And the love we share with our family and friends
Is the tie that will bind us far beyond the end.

Have hope and you know God's promise will hold true.
Learn love's not only what you feel but what you say and do.
Find faith to be your sight for things you cannot see
And rest assured my friend; I'll see you again in Eternity.

Although we don't know how our future will be
Have faith that God has a plan for you
And like me it may not be the way you hoped it would turn out.
But just remember that He loves you and if you're ever in doubt...

Have hope and you know God's promise will hold true.
Learn love's not only what you feel but what you say and do.
Find faith to be your sight for things you cannot see
And rest assured my friend; I'll see you again in Eternity.

Janeen Williams

I dedicate this song to my Mother who was wise enough to know that weekly worship, Sunday School, and other church activities would be the foundation on which my faith and relationship with God would be built — a relationship I would draw strength and comfort from all my life.

Everlasting Faith

When I look upon your face
And I see the strength that you've displayed
I can only be amazed
And go out into the world and spread the faith
Seasons change and as life goes on we look to you
And this remains; there will always be
Your Everlasting Faith

Paul Skowron

Faith

In this walk with Jesus
Many faulty steps I've trodden
Where would I be
Without the grace of God?

Leo Feher

On behalf of our board of directors, we would like to thank several people who made this possible.

We first would like to recognize our famlies and friends for their unbelievable support. The others who have "A Way With Words". The associate editor Vicki Matthews, who organized, typed and computerized the book. The community near Austintown, Ohio and the customers and friends of Glorious Homes, Inc. Their contributions were so valuable concerning this project. Also the talent and genuine compassion of Phil Baden (publisher). His abilities and dedication gave this book wings.

Thanks to everyone!

Index
Alphabetically by Author

Barrett, Marvin C. .Grandma's House 40

. . . . .My Country Girl 45

. . . . .Sweetheart in Dreamland 67

. . . . .The Doctor's Wife 23

Bromley, Sandy . . . . .Life is Too Short to Wear Beige Pants 17

. . . . .Yankee Pride 20

. . . . .The Tomato 58

Campbell, Judith . . . . .Body Mold 62

Dietz, Kaitlyn . . . . .The Survivor's Life Saver 33

Feher, Leo . . . . .Faith 83

Fithian, Will & Theo Kennisten . . . . .Allie 77

Gianoglio, Ron . . . . .Clear The Air 71

Gilmartin, Thomas P. Sr. . . . . . .Art Show Colors Everywhere 53

. . . . .Holding Hands 55

Hayes, Louis . . . . .Dreams, Thoughts, Plans and Actions 75

Hill, Hilliary . . . . .A Special Gift 72

Labuda, Charlotte Louise . . . . .Inspiration 57

. . . . .The Rock 42

. . . . .Where's Maga 64

Matthews, Eric & Vicki . . . . .Brenda 43

Matthews, Vicki . . . . .Together 66

McClellan, Eric . . . . .Someone's Watching 80

Neidlinger, Lori . . . . .Dandelions Roar 32

Rider, Brenda . . . . Angels Without Wings 24
. . . . Artist of the Spirit 27
. . . . Best Nurse 26
. . . . Birthday To Birthday 16
. . . . Blessings 2
. . . . Christmas 2004 37
. . . . Circle of Friends 4
. . . . Classic Autumn Leaves 52
. . . . For a Moment 56
. . . . Future 12
. . . . Generation Bridge 47
. . . . Hope In What We Do 28
. . . . Light of a Child 34
. . . . Lighthouse of Hope 25
. . . . My Friend 46
. . . . Natures Way 15
. . . . One Day 6
. . . . Picked Up a Smile 48
. . . . Rainbow of Ribbons 76
. . . . Relay for Life 8
. . . . Relay the Message 74
. . . . Remarkable Child 35
. . . . Remember October 3
. . . . Right Reasons 22
. . . . Roses For Life 7
. . . . Seeds For The Mountain 54
. . . . Tears To Keep 5
. . . . To a Yankee FAN-NY 20
. . . . What is a Sister? 44
. . . . When Horses Run And Eagles Fly 13
. . . . Within You 14

Schaffert, Karen L.	To My Father	63
Skowron, Paul	Everlasting Faith	82
	Jessica	78
Ula, Tristan	One Step at a Time	68
Williams, Janeen	Eternity	81
Woodford, Debbie	The Token Song	70
Zackeroff, Martha	Special Place	36
	Walk Gently	65